How Catholics
Won
Protestant Respect

How Catholics Won Protestant Respect
A Candid Look at America

PETER FIELDS

The Hermit Kingdom Press
Cheltenham ♦ Seoul ♦ Bangalore ♦ Cebu

HOW CATHOLICS WON PROTESTANT RESPECT: A CANDID LOOK AT AMERICA

ISBN 1-59689-041-X (paperback)
ISBN 1-59689-042-8 (Adobe ebook)

Write-To Address:

The Hermit Kingdom Press
3741 Walnut Street, Suite 407
Philadelphia, PA 19104
United States of America

Info@TheHermitKingdomPress.com

★ ★ ★ ★

Hermit Kingdom
12 South Bridge, Suite 370
Edinburgh, EH1 1DD
Scotland

http://www.TheHermitKingdomPress.com

Dedicated to Every Christian in America

Contents

"If the Supreme Court says that you have the right to consensual gay sex within your home, then you have the right to bigamy, you have the right to polygamy, you have the right to incest, you have the right to adultery. You have the right to anything."

U.S. Senator Rick Santorum
A Roman-Catholic Republican

Introduction

In Philadelphia, two Roman Catholic churches were burned down while Catholics were worshipping inside. Thankfully, most were able to get out without any injury. Philadelphia is not an isolated case. Roman Catholics suffered in America for many decades.

It is true that the Protestants who delivered suffering to Catholics were probably Protestants in name only and were not active, practicing Christians. However, it is true to say that Roman Catholics had the hardest time getting respect in America, which is a Christian nation dominated by Protestants.

When I was growing up and going to a Christian high school that was evangelical Protestant in nature, I remember that most of my classmates did not have any Catholic friends. It was understood that marrying a Catholic was a no-no.

But it was not just from the Protestant side. Catholics were not interested in marrying Protestants, by in large. To be married in a Catholic church, the parents had to promise to raise their children Catholic. Catholics thought that it was best to marry a Catholic and some even believed that it was not possible to get Protestants to sign on the dotted line to raise their children Catholic.

And Catholics in America have worked hard to provide Catholic education for their children, grandchildren, and posterity. There are Catholic universities all over America. And every major US city has a very active and extensive Catholic school system from kindergarten to high school. There is the capacity for every Catholic who wants to be educated Catholic to receive Catholic education.

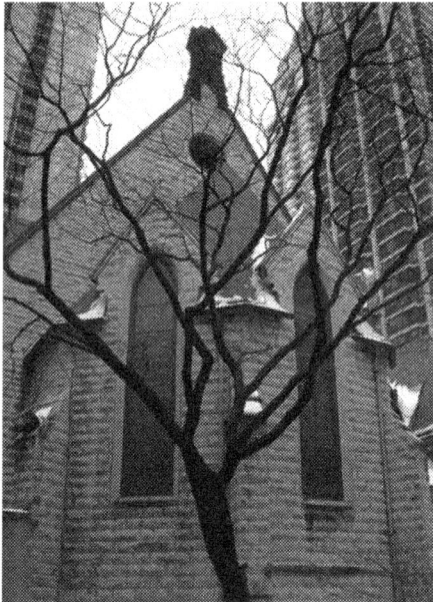

It was not easy for Roman Catholics to raise a Catholic educational infrastructure from ground up. Many Catholics toiled and worked very, very hard. After shedding much blood-sweat at hard labor jobs, many Catholics gave money to the church to raise up a Catholic educational infrastructure for their posterity. The Catholic educational system is a testimony to the sacrifice and hard work of Catholics in American history. Needless to say, Catholic education is valued in the Catholic community.

In the same way, Protestants have worked hard to provide Christian education for their children. There are Christian universities of Protestant persuasion all over the United States. The most prominent Protestant Christian colleges are Wheaton College in Illinois, Calvin College in Michigan, Bob Jones University in South Carolina, Oral Roberts University in Oklahoma, and Liberty University in Virginia.

Although not as elaborate as the Catholic parochial system, Protestant Christians have set up Christian schools all over the United States, from kindergarten to high school. These Christian schools are generally one hundred percent Protestant Christian in student, faculty, and staff composition. They are generally tied to a church or a Christian denomination and actively inculcate students in the teachings of the church.

Socially, it is easy to see how, for instance, in the city of Chicago, Protestants and Catholics can live a few blocks apart but experience a completely different social group through the educational systems set up by their churches.

And religion is very important for most Americans. It is not difficult to see when we realize that America was founded for religious reasons. Puritans were kicked out of England by Anglicans and started America. Puritans, therefore, had a chip on their shoulders and aggressively pushed Puritan education. The emphasis on religious education rubbed off on everyone who came to America.

The emphasis on religion is not found just in the origins of America. In the historical storytelling and worldview of Americans today, a distinctive nostalgic look at America's Christian origins can be seen. Many Americans simply assume that the American Founding Fathers were Christians and were interested in having a Christian America. For many Americans, this idea has taken a folk status. In other words, regardless of historical accuracy, Americans have a collective memory or perception of the past American history in religious terms.

Perhaps because religion is important and perceived as important by almost every American, religious education occupies a prominent place in American society.

When George W. Bush and Al Gore were fighting for the US President position in 2000, both of them supported using government funds to help Christian churches with their social and/or educational programs. Religion is very important to Americans and is becoming increasingly important in American politics.

Both Catholics and Protestants are dedicated to the idea of a Christian America. Historically, they have set up different educational and social institutions to achieve their goals.

Perhaps, it is the force of the Reformation of Luther that has kept Protestants from actively approaching

Catholics to build a Christian America together in the past. It could be the fact that the Vatican has historically discouraged recognizing Protestant Christians as active partners in the Kingdom of Christ that may have played a role. Whatever may have been the reason, Protestants and Catholics have in the past not worked as closely together to build a Christian America, while both practicing Catholics and practicing Protestants, by in large, wanted the same thing ultimately.

Given that there have always been far more Protestants than Catholics, when there was a social conflict, Catholics suffered. Of course, social conflicts were fuelled by misunderstandings and often instigated by those who forgot the similarities between Catholics and Protestants.

Protestants and Catholics share all the major ecumenical councils in the 2,000 years of Christian history that are fundamental to the understanding of Jesus Christ and the Trinity. Protestants and Catholics agree on many of the core points of what is important in life and life thereafter.

But not all Protestants studied what Catholics believe, and not all

Catholics studied what Protestants believe. So, there was much misunderstanding and a lot of conflicts rose out of misunderstanding.

Perhaps out of lack of enough information, many Protestants looked down on Catholics historically in America. There is a reason why the United States only had one Roman Catholic President in US history. It is not a coincidence.

It seems, however, that Protestants in America are changing their minds. Protestants are showing evidence of genuine respect for Catholics. There have been no active calls by Protestant leaders to respect Catholics. Nobody is putting guns to Protestant heads and telling them to respect Catholics. No one is threatening to fire anyone from his job for not respecting Catholics.

So, what has changed? Why do Protestant Christians respect Catholic Christians now?

Perhaps, the answer can be found in key social policies that Roman Catholics push in the American social and political scenes. Namely, they are prohibitions in the following areas: abortion, pre-marital sex, and homosexuality.

It is to these social policies that we now turn.

Abortion

To say that abortion does not matter in American politics is like saying that people do not need oxygen. Abortion has played a key role in American politics in the past few decades. Political candidates have lost their victory because of their support of abortion.

Some argue that John Kerry, a Roman Catholic, lost the US Presidential race because he supported pro-abortion legislation. Roman Catholics defected and voted for George W. Bush who supports anti-abortion legislation.

Perhaps, the fact that Pope John Paul II declared in an official papal pronouncement that Roman Catholics around the world must oppose and vote against political candidates who support pro-abortion legislation played a role. Even in those Democrat states comprised of Roman Catholics that John Kerry won, he won by a margin of less than 5 percent in many cases. It is clear that many Roman Catholics defected and voted for Bush, who is an evangelical Protestant Christian.

It goes without saying that abortion plays a major role in American politics. Pope John Paul II has made abortion the most important issue of the Roman Catholic Church. The anti-abortion position of the Roman Catholic Church shows the Vatican to be in-genious. It portrayed Roman Catholics as fighters for the lives of unborn children.

With ultrasound imaging, it has become increasingly difficult for the proponents of abortion to say that a fetus is not a live child. Roman Catholics won the moral fight on scientific grounds.

From the standpoint of the attitude of Protestant Christians, the ag-gressive anti-abortion position of Roman Catholics and the Vatican has encour-aged respect.

It would be highly accurate to say that now when Protestant Christians think about Roman Catholics, they think of people who oppose abortion and pro-abortion legislation. This perception has encouraged deep respect of Catholics as protectors of innocent life.

It's not surprising that Roman Catholics have stamped themselves as champions of innocent, unborn life. Most American universities have a New-man Center. The Newman Center at a university is a Catholic student organi-zation and chaplaincy. The Newman Center acts as the center of Catholic re-ligious and social life at a university.

The Newman Center provides Catholic education, Bible studies, and religious programs for Catholic students on campus. The Newman Center also emphasizes values that are important to Catholic Christians. One of the most im-portant values among Catholics is to oppose abortion. The Newman Center at any given university in America, there-fore, teaches about abortion and en-courages active anti-abortion stance among students attending the university. In many cases, the Newman Center organizes big anti-abortion rallies. Some have been known to organize more than one major anti-abortion rally per se-mester. More often than not, the

Newman Center plays an instrumental leadership role in a secular university to organize anti-abortion rallies and lectures.

The critical role played by Newman Centers all over the United States has not gone unnoticed. Largely Protestant Christian groups, such as the Campus Crusades for Christ (CCC), the Navigators, and the Inter-Varsity Christian Fellowship (IVCF) have come to respect the Newman Center particularly for its leadership role in organizing anti-abortion rallies.

Many Protestant Christian groups even made active alliances with the Newman Center on secular college campuses to fight abortion. The University of Pennsylvania, for instance, saw such an alliance come alive in 1989. Many American secular universities saw the reality of alliance of Protestant Christians and Catholic Christians to fight abortion. By in large, the reason for the fight is similar, with Jesus Christ being an important element in the argument against abortion.

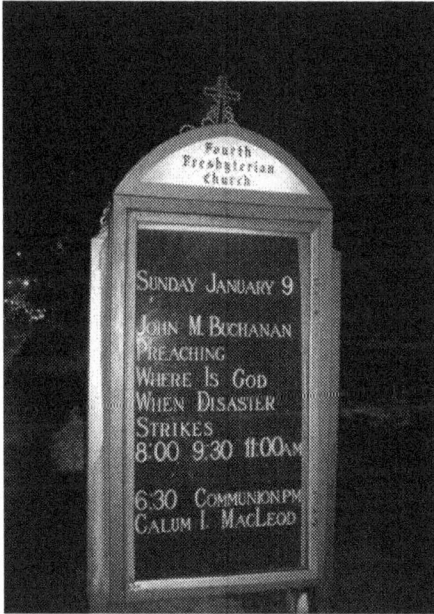

Because the Newman Center is often unabashedly public and aggressive in its anti-abortion program, American

Protestant Christians at the university have come to respect them.

The force of conviction is generally respectable, so even liberal Protestants who may not necessarily agree with the exact position of the Newman Center came to respect the center and the Catholics on campus. Of course, practicing Protestant Christians who are actively against abortion naturally came to respect the Newman Center and campus Catholics not only for their strong convictions but their effective strategy to push an anti-abortion agenda publicly on campus and in university discourse.

Like in the university setting with the Newman Center, America's Catholics have proven themselves to be effective organizers and moral voice against abortion in the general American society and public settings. Many Catholic churches organize or help organize anti-abortion rallies and/or anti-abortion lobbying on local, state, and national levels.

These efforts of America's Catholic Christians have not gone unnoticed by Protestant Christians. Protestant Christians have come to respect Roman Catholics for their active role in social, political, and public life to protect lives of innocent unborn children.

It is not surprising to see why Catholic Christians fighting against abortion became a source to bring respect for Catholics. America's Protestant Christians have come to privilege fight against abortion as an important element of their identity as Christians. Protecting innocent unborn life became an important ethical concern that quickly became one of the most important American Protestant Christian ethics.

Unlike Catholic Christian protest against abortion, Protestant Christian opposition to abortion sometimes became violent. It is not unusual to hear about European comics poking fun of some Fundamentalist Christians bombing an abortion clinic and killing doctors who perform abortions.

Although Fundamentalist Christians do not necessarily condone such violent protest against abortion performers, it is not too surprising if you follow the rationale of those who act. Without condoning their actions, let's unpack their reasoning. They believe that abortion is murdering children. Because abortion is killing innocent, helpless children, doctors who perform abortions are killing children. They reason that it is important to stop the killing, so they kill whom they see as the murderer of children.

There are some in the Protestant Christian circles who take matters into their own hands because they genuinely believe that protecting innocent lives is important enough to go to jail. In their defense (since they generally never get a fair hearing), it should be stated that they probably are the kind of people who would try to protect the innocent from murderers, such as oppressive despots. They would be willing to risk their life and time in jail to protect innocent lives from harm or death.

Catholic anti-abortion movement has been peaceful, by in large. America's Catholics hold public protests and demonstrations. America's Catholics try to fight abortion in the courts and through legislation. America's Catholics are organized in supporting anti-abortion candidates for public office.

Perhaps because local, state-wide, and national Catholic structures already exist, America's Catholic Christians were able to give vent to their anti-abortion sentiments through the existent structures.

For Protestant Christians, this was not easily possible at first. Protestant Christians do not always have very effective local, state, and national structures – and certainly, there wasn't any structure to formalize resistance to abortion through church bodies at first. Even now, most Protestant Christian churches do not integrate anti-abortion protest into their church structure. Protestant Christians have been slow (certainly in comparison to Catholic Christians) to organize as a group against abortion. This may explain why some individual Protestant Christians have resorted to violence to stop the killing of babies.

Protestant Christians have now developed some nationwide organizations to fight abortion. They tend to be broadly evangelical Christian – since evangelical Christianity is a movement across many Protestant Christian denominations, like the Baptists, Methodists, Assemblies of God, and Presbyterians. These nation-wide anti-abortion Christian movements were started often by concerned lay individuals, rather than church leaders in Protestant Christian church structures.

Precisely because Protestant Christians have been slow to mount a public resistance against abortion and abortion legislation, many anti-abortion tending Protestant Christians came to respect the work of the Roman Catholic Church and its nationwide structures.

In fact, at first when Protestant Christians wanted to join an anti-abortion rally they had to join the one sponsored by the Roman Catholic Church or one of its agencies. In many cases, there was no other Christian option. It is easy to see how anti-abortion Protestant Christians came to respect the Roman Catholic Church for quickly adapting their system to fight abortion in public and through politics.

In fact, many Protestant Christian organizations that were formed to oppose abortion modelled their programs after established programs of Roman Catholics. What they did was to organize Protestant Christians against abortion in the way that the Roman Catholic Church and Catholic organizations did with America's Catholics.

The anti-abortion fight of America's Catholics brought them respect. The respect of America's Protestant Christians who looked down on them for centuries which could not have been bought with money or wealth was earned through the Catholic Christian struggle against abortion.

Now, many Protestant Christian anti-abortion agencies work closely with Catholic Christian anti-abortion agencies to fight abortion, pro-abortion legislation, and abortion supporting politicians.

Protestant Christians have found commonality in the anti-abortion struggle. And this common purpose is facilitated by the growing realization that Catholic Christians and Protestant Christians share a very important common ground – namely, faith in Jesus Christ as God and the belief that God is in three persons – God the Father, God the Son, and God the Holy Spirit.

Pre-Marital Sex

When people think about Catholic schools, people often think about austere nuns who teach in Catholic schools. Although popular media often caricature this picture, many Catholic Christians are proud of the fact that great Catholic Christian education is provided by very dedicated Christian leaders. Catholic parents spend thousands of dollars of their hard-earned cash to send their children to Catholic schools because they know that dedicated Catholic Christians will bring up their children with a good Catholic Christian education.

Nuns are certainly dedicated Christians. It is difficult to take a vow of celibacy. It takes great commitment and love of Jesus Christ to take that step. Nuns have done so and committed themselves in celibacy for the Kingdom of Christ.

The Roman Catholic Church has always respected the value of celibacy for Christ's sake. It was seen as a special gift of the Holy Spirit.

And the Roman Catholic Church always perceived sex not as something to give humans pleasure but rather as something to bring glory to God. Thus, sex was confined to marriage, and marriage was for the sake of forming a Christian family to bring glory to God.

The Roman Catholic Church has a very elaborate and developed teaching on the concept of Christian marriage, Christian family, and sex within the confines of a marriage before God.

And the Roman Catholic Church and Catholic schools are serious about teaching their young the Christian principles about sex within the confines of marriage – which certainly means no pre-marital sex.

The fact that dedicated Catholic Christians, like nuns, participate in the teaching process ensures that the important teaching of the Roman Catholic

Church becomes centralized in its teaching and Bible study curriculum.

The Christian church has historically emphasized sex in the context of marriage. Besides the Biblical teaching, the Roman Catholic Church's respect for Virgin Mary further propels their prohibition against pre-marital sex.

Virgin Mary is respected because she was a virgin even when she was engaged to be married. This is often used as a lesson for teaching that a Catholic must not have sex even when he or she is engaged. Sex should only be done after the bond of holy matrimony.

Jesus Christ was conceived in the Virgin's womb by the power of the Holy Spirit. This was essential for Jesus Christ to be born sinless. No Protestant would have a problem with this teaching of the Roman Catholic Church. Indeed, both Protestant Christians and Catholic Christians are fundamentally agreed in the importance of emphasizing the virginity of Mary at the time of the work of the Holy Spirit in her womb.

The Roman Catholic Church has historically given Virgin Mary a more exalted place than a typical Protestant church and this may be the reason why the Roman Catholic Church has a greater emphasis on virginity.

Currently, Hispanics are considered the largest ethnic minority in the United States. Majority of the Hispanics in America are Roman Catholics (the rest tend to be very conservative charismatic Christians). Hispanic Catholics are extremely conservative on the issue of pre-marital sex. Although there is greater emphasis for virginity at the family level among Hispanic Catholics, all Catholics in America believe in the principle that people should remain virgins before they get married. Certainly, the Roman Catholic Church and Catholic schools teach this as the official position.

The radical emphasis on prohibiting pre-marital sex among Catholics has won respect from Protestant Christians in America.

America's Protestant Christian churches came to respect the Roman Catholic Church's consistency in prohibiting pre-marital sex officially and publicly as many Protestant Christians felt that pre-marital sexual practices were proliferating dangerously.

Many Protestant Christians came increasingly worried about their children in an increasingly promiscuous culture. Perhaps, it would not be wrong to say that there is something very American about desiring to protect the innocence particularly of children.   There are decency laws in America. One of the reasons why it is illegal to consume alcohol openly in public in America (and you can get arrested and sent to jail for this) is the social concern that the young might be tempted and tainted. Giving alcohol to a minor is a big offense in America and one can go to jail for this.

Efforts to shield the young from sexual promiscuity and temptation are one of the reasons why having sex in a public place is a prosecutable offense. America is overprotective when it comes to efforts to protect the morality of the young, and American laws clearly show this.

People in the world are aware of what happened in the 2004 Superbowl half-time show when Janet Jackson's top was torn and her breast was exposed. It has come to be known as "wardrobe malfunction." For that, the TV station was fined a lot of money by government regulators. Many businesses actually pulled their advertisement out and the TV station ended up losing millions of dollars. Most Americans and the American government are concerned about protecting the young from sexual and moral degeneration. This is an important part of the American cultural scene.

Protestant Christians often take active and concrete steps. American Protestant Christians argue that sex is only for marriage. As such, many American Protestant Christian churches officially and even actively prohibit pre-marital sex.

Even in the most liberal of the mainline Protestant Christian churches in America, it is safe to assume that they will discourage pre-marital sex.

Among evangelical Protestant Christians, who comprise the majority of America's Christians (some estimate at 150 million of the American people or about 50 percent of the population), pre-marital sex is actively and overtly discouraged at every turn.

47

Major evangelical universities, like Biola University in Southern California and Wheaton College, have required its students to sign a statement saying that they will not drink even a sip of alcohol. There is the understanding that consumption of alcohol leads to pre-marital sex because it lowers moral guards. Traditionally, these schools have discouraged dancing for the same reasons. Most Protestant Christian high schools in America ban dances on the same account. They want to do all they can to discourage pre-marital sex.

Some Protestant Christians, like those at Bob Jones University, prohibit going to watch a movie in a movie theatre because they believe that it can encourage pre-marital sex. Many Protestant Christians in America try to help the young not be in a context where they may be tempted to breach their innocence and commit pre-marital sex.

Josh McDowell is a leading teacher on Christian dating. His books are the standard at many Protestant Christian churches for youth group instruction. Josh McDowell clearly takes the position against pre-marital sex. The title of his popular book tells it all: *Why True Love Waits: A Definitive*

Book on How to Help Your Youth Resist Sexual Pressure. Josh McDowell tries to dispel the notion that just because you feel strongly for someone, you should have sex with them. Josh McDowell, like most evangelical Christian leaders in America, emphasizes the principle that pre-marital sex is absolutely wrong.

Among America's Protestant Christians, there is a movement to take an oath of virginity. Christians in junior high school and in high school are encouraged by church leaders and Christian school leaders to sign a document stating that they promise before God to remain virgins until they get married.

The oath of virginity is meant to impress the seriousness of the Christian prohibition against pre-marital sex. It is clear how serious America's Protestant Christians are about combating promiscuous pre-marital sex and public corruption of the young.

Many Protestant Christians approach virginity until marriage and prohibition against pre-marital sex a little bit differently than America's Catholic Christians. While both Protestant Christians and Catholic Christians agree that Christianity prohibits pre-marital sex and that churches should uphold this important principle of the Bible, America's Protestant Christians focus on the concept of holiness as a reason for why Christians must not engage in pre-marital sex.

Protestant Christians argue that the Triune God of the Old Testament and the New Testament demands that Christians try to imitate His holiness.

The emphasis on holiness and opposing sexual immorality is clear in the Bible. 1 Thessalonians 4:3-7 states:

It is God's will that you should be sanctified: that you should avoid sexual immorality; that each of you should learn to control his own body in a way that is holy and honourable, not in passionate lust like the heathen, who do not know God; and that in this matter none should wrong his brother or take advantage of him. The Lord will punish men for all such sins, as we have already told you and warned you. For God did not call us to be impure, but to live a holy life.

Most Protestant Christian churches in America would say that sexual immorality being described includes pre-marital sex. Engaging in pre-marital sex is wrong because it is against God's instructions for sexual purity. Sexual purity is an important part of imitating the holiness of the Triune God.

Of course, the Roman Catholic Church would recognize the importance of this Bible passage and other Bible passages demanding sexual purity. However, the Holiness movement impacted America's Protestants in a strong way. The Fundamentalist movement of early 1900's is a testimony to the impact that the Holiness movement had among America's Protestant Christians. Even today, the Holiness movement is an important part of American Protestant Christianity.

It is, therefore, not wrong to say that prohibition against pre-marital sex is an integral part of the American Protestant Christian understanding on holiness, the God of the Bible, and Christian identity.

Because opposing pre-marital sex in principle is so important to the majority of American Protestant Christians, it is easy to see why they would develop respect for the Roman Catholic Church.

The Roman Catholic Church is just as aggressive, if not more aggressive, than a typical American Protestant church in emphasizing that pre-marital sex is wrong.

American Protestant Christians came to respect the Roman Catholic Church and America's Catholics more and more as they saw how much Catholic education was tied to prohibiting pre-marital sex.

The respect comes not only from the vantage point of shared Christian values. America's Protestant Christians genuinely respect the fact that America's Roman Catholics were able to build an elaborate infrastructure to emphasize that pre-marital sex is wrong. It shows an impressive organizational skill to further the principles of the Kingdom of Christ. The extensive Catholic parochial system inculcates the Christian value of prohibition of pre-marital sex.

Furthermore, Catholic Christian youth movements are being organized on local, state, and national levels. All these Catholic Christian youth movements emphasize the prohibition on pre-marital sex.

America's Protestant Christians appreciate the Catholic Christian efforts to make America a holier Christian nation.

Like the Puritans before them, most American Christians want to see America as a Christian nation with responsibilities as a Christian nation. Most American Protestant Christians see Christians as God's chosen people. They believe that there is a responsibility to being a chosen people.

The Vatican II clearly emphasizes that Christians are God's chosen people. In this emphasis, therefore, Protestant Christians and Catholic

Christians are agreed. The active work to prohibit pre-marital sex by America's Catholics encourages American Protestant Christians to see them as kindred spirits and fellow members of the chosen people of God to work for a Christian America.

Homosexuality

American Protestant Christians have come to respect Catholic Christians because of their effective opposition to abortion and pre-marital sex. More recently, American Protestant Christians have come to respect Catholic Christians for another thing – namely, the Catholic Christian condemnation of homosexuality.

For 2,000 years, the Roman Catholic Church has been consistent in condemning homosexuality. The condemnation of homosexuality is not surprising in light of the Bible and is in agreement with the teaching of the Bible – both the Old Testament and the New Testament.

The Old Testament is clear in condemning homosexuality. Leviticus 18:22 states: "Do not lie with a man as one lies with a woman; that is detestable." The Leviticus passage condemns homosexuality. Sexual intercourse is condemned; more importantly, it is necessary to note that sleeping together (even without sexual intercourse) is condemned.

The Old Testament considers homosexuality as such a serious offense that the Old Testament shows God as justified in completely annihilating a populace because of homosexuality. Genesis 19 accounts how God annihilated everyone in Sodom and Gomorrah except for Lot's family. It is clear that the people in Sodom and Gomorrah actively practiced homosexuality. In fact, homosexuality was so prevalent that when the angel of the LORD came to visit Lot, the townspeople were interested in gang-homosexual-raping him (Genesis 19:4-5). Lot is portrayed as a righteous man because he prevents the homosexual rape (Genesis 19:6-9). In a sense, the Bible is showing why God was right in saving Lot and his family.

In Genesis 19, homosexual practices and a communal depravity that allows homosexual rape are the reasons why God was seen as righteous in completely destroying the cities and every living thing in them. God saved the one who opposed homosexual rape – he was implicitly seen as the righteous one.

The teaching against homosexuality plays a prominent role in the New Testament as well. Romans1:24-27 states:

> *Because of this, God gave them over to shameful lusts. Even their women exchanged natural relations for unnatural ones. In the same way the men also abandoned natural relations with women and were inflamed with lust for one another. Men committed indecent acts with other men, and received in themselves the due penalty for their perversion.*

The New Testament is clear in emphasizing that homosexuality is an abomination to God. Furthermore, homosexuality is seen as unnatural. In other words, it goes against nature to engage in homosexuality. Thus, killing would be a sin, but a natural sin. In contrast, committing homosexuality is far worse because it is an unnatural sin and goes against the natural, created order.

It is understandable in this light why God would not annihilate a city and kill all living thing in a city for murder that is committed, but God would destroy a city completely and kill everything in a city for the wickedness of homosexuality which condones homosexual rape even of a servant of God.

Romans 1 promises that there is a "due penalty" for homosexuality. The New Testament explains homosexuality explicitly as a very serious offense.

Both the Old Testament and the New Testament are clear in condemning homosexuality as completely abominable before God – and as something that God will certainly punish.

The Roman Catholic Church has been in agreement with the Bible for 2,000 years certainly in the active condemnation of homosexuality. Pope John Paul II has gone on official record as saying that homosexual marriage is one of the greatest evils in the world today.

Pope John Paul II has condemned homosexual marriage with greater zeal than he has genocides or other cruel acts of human history. Pope John Paul II proved that he is in keeping with the Bible. The Bible never condemned genocides as such, but the Bible clearly condemns homosexuality. Pope John Paul II is being a faithful servant of the Triune God in his proactive opposition to homosexuality – the unnatural sin of abomination.

America's Protestant Christians have not failed to take notice. There may be a few – a negligible few – who have jumped on the political correctness bandwagon, but majority of American Protestant Christians consider homosexuality as an unnatural sin. And even many of those few who may have jumped on the political correctness bandwagon will never think of practicing homosexuality themselves or would desire anyone they know to practise it. They are merely on a political correctness intellectual trip.

Particularly in the American context, homosexuality is seen as something that is detestable. It's not only among the Christian population. Even non-Christians think this way. Right now, President George W. Bush is trying to make a US Constitutional amendment to ban homosexual marriage. This would bar any pro-homosexuality legislation from passing for the foreseeable future. President George W. Bush's plan seems to jive with the sentiment of the American people.

Some 17 states have voted to make amendments to their state constitutions to bar homosexual marriage. No laws can be passed in these 17 states to support homosexuality. In the next couple of years, some 20 states or more are predicted to make similar constitutional amendments to their state constitution. All the states which have put the amendment on the ballot won with a wide margin of popular support. The American people want to see homosexual marriage permanently banned, and many people are fighting on local, state, and national levels to bring this about. It is not a mistake to state that this represents the ethos of the American people.

This reality in America is understandable for any American who lives in

America. It is common knowledge in America that if you as a man grab a man's butt in a club, you should not be surprised to be beaten to a pulp or even killed. Two men walking hand-in-hand even in the streets of San Francisco can reasonably expect to be beaten up. This is America and American culture.

Of course, people inflicting the violence may not be practicing Christians. But Christians will feel the same kind of disgust at homosexuality that their more violent American compatriots may feel (and act on). Certainly, Christianity condemns homosexuality as an abomination and recognizes God's right to annihilate a place that gives approval of unfettered homosexual practices and of homosexual rape without recrimination.

The difference, of course, is in the reason of opposition. Christians oppose homosexuality because they fear God and God's punishment. Christians oppose homosexuality because the Bible teaches that it is an unnatural sin that God will certainly punish without mercy.

Non-Christians oppose homosexuality because of the conscience that God has given to them or because they perceive that it will degenerate society and it will not be good for them in the long run. Maybe some non-Christians act violently toward homosexuals because they are disgusted at homosexual advances or efforts to spread homosexuality. Perhaps they perceive something in "homosexual immorality" that they see as immediately detrimental to society.

Whatever the difference in the reasons for opposing homosexuality, majority of Americans are united in the opposition to homosexuality.

But even if majority of Americans were not opposed to homosexuality, practising Christians would be because the ban on homosexuality in the Bible is very clear.

For most Protestant Christians, active teaching against homosexuality is a very important part of being a Christian. A church is required to resist proliferation of homosexuality in a society because just like Sodom and Gomorrah, proliferation of homosexuality and immorality attached to homosexuality can be the reason for God choosing to annihilate your society and every living thing in it.

Protestant Christians in America believe that the Triune God of the Bible actually exists and that He has the power to destroy everything He wants. Thus, Protestant Christians have a healthy fear of the Triune God of the Bible and respect for Him.

It is possible to say that opposing homosexuality is an integral part of being an evangelical Protestant Christian in America.

It is understandable in light of all this why America's Protestant Christians have developed respect for Roman Catholics. The Roman Catholic Church has consistently opposed homosexuality for the whole of past 2,000 years. In other words, there was never a period in the whole history of the Roman Catholic Church when it did not actively attack homosexuality. This fact is something that America's Protestant Christians can respect.

Furthermore, the Roman Catholic Church is aggressive about attacking homosexuality and homosexual marriage at the present. As mentioned before, Pope John Paul II considers homosexual marriage as one of the greatest evil in the world.

What's more, many Catholic Christians in America follow the Christian lead of the Vatican and accept the Biblical teaching against homosexuality.

In many cases, prominent Roman Catholic leaders in American public and social life have unabashedly spoken out against homosexuality. Many Protestant Christians were watching and came to respect the courage in defending the Christian faith.

For example, US Senator from Pennsylvania, Rick Santorum said in an interview with Associated Press: "If the Supreme Court says that you have the right to consensual gay sex within your home, then you have the right to bigamy, you have the right to polygamy, you have the right to incest, you have the right to adultery. You have the right to anything." Senator Rick Santorum is a Roman Catholic Christian.

It certainly took courage for Senator Santorum to say what he said. When Senator Santorum publicly declared his position against homosexuality, he put many Protestant Christians to shame because they agreed with Senator Santorum but they realized that they lacked the courage to say that in public – in the open.

Senator Santorum is the only non-clergy Roman Catholic Christian who opposed homosexuality openly and publicly. There are other Roman Catholic Christian social leaders who have braved political correctness police to air their Christian beliefs. This makes a lot of ordinary Protestant Christians to respect Catholic Christians.

Senator Santorum took a risk in saying what he said in affirming his belief and that is why he earned the respect of many people.

An influential group, Concerned Women for America, based in Washington, DC, publicly commented that Senator Santorum was "exactly right." Their opinion represents the general opinion of many influential political groups in Washington, DC.

The Family Research Council commented that if candidates want to receive more votes they should be as open as Senator Santorum about their anti-homosexuality position. The suggestion by the Family Research Council certainly makes a lot of sense in the American context. Some 17 states passed an amendment to their state constitution to ban homosexual marriage. Studies after studies have shown that the majority of Americans think of homosexuality as detestable and destructive to society.

It is surprising that not many more have openly declared their position against homosexuality. A part of the reason is fear, of course. There are aggressive pro-homosexuality lobby groups that are bound to give you hard time. And there are enough political correctness police-types out there that a

social or political leader may be afraid of
political repercussions.

But all the indicators are there
that the time is right for political and
social leaders to declare their positions
against homosexuality without much
problem.

What is respectful about Catholic
Christians – in the minds of Protestant
Christians – is that they came out and
declared their anti-homosexuality positions before clear indicators were there
that they would not get into trouble.

The Roman Catholic Church has
acted in such a manner. Pope John Paul
II declared homosexual marriage as a
great evil without worrying about
repercussions of his statement. Pope

John Paul II was concerned about upholding the principles of the Bible. This is something that America's Protestant Christians respect.

Certainly, homosexuality is one of the important reasons why Catholics gained Protestant respect in the United States.

Conclusion

Catholics have successfully gained Protestant respect in America. Protestant Christians respect the fact that Catholic Christians actively oppose abortion, pre-marital sex, and homosexuality. What's more, the Roman Catholic Church has built up an elaborate and integrated structure within America to mount their offensive against abortion, pre-marital sex, and homosexuality.

Individual Catholic Christians have often been courageous in their standing up for the principles of Christianity. For this, they have won respect of America's Protestant Christians.

But the respect that the Roman Catholic Church and Catholics in America enjoy is not permanent. It all depends on Catholics continuing to uphold Christian principles and proving again and again that they are courageous and brave. To maintain American Protestant respect for the Roman Catholic Church and Catholic Christians, America's Catholics have to continue to prove that they are effective in opposing abortion, pre-marital sex, and homosexuality. It is an on-going struggle. It is a never ending fight.

Fortunately for the Roman Catholic Church and America's Catholics, the struggle against abortion, pre-marital sex, and homosexuality is an integral part of what being a Catholic Christian is. And the Catholic Christian social struggle will continue.

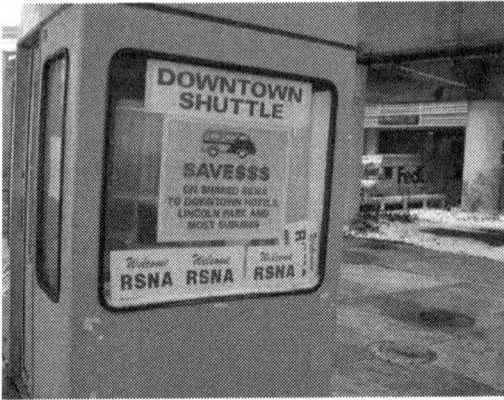

As long as the Roman Catholic Church and America's Catholics fight the good fight on behalf of the Christian Triune God, they will continue to win more and more Protestant Christians over to respecting them.

Of course, many Catholic Christians fight abortion, pre-marital sex, and homosexuality not because they want respect from America's Protestant Christians, but because it is the right thing to do. The Roman Catholic Church is struggling for the Kingdom of Christ and the Word of God. However, winning Protestant Christian respect is an added bonus.

Perhaps, the 21st century will be a golden age for America's Protestant Christians and Catholic Christians to work together for a Christian America. There are many challenges facing America, and it would be nice for all true Christians to work together to make

America a more Christian country and a
better place for all as a result.

I do have some suggestions for a
more active cooperation of true Christians. Both Protestant Christians and
Catholic Christians should be united in
declaring that Jesus Christ is the only
way to salvation. As the belief that
Jesus Christ is God and the true Savior is
central to Christianity, it should be

brought out to the front. It is the Biblical truth that Protestant Christians and Catholic Christians can agree on. Public declaration together will give Christian efforts a sense of purpose and meaning.

With a shared sense of Christian destiny, Protestant Christians and Catholic Christians can walk together through thin and think, through cold and hot, and glorify Jesus Christ together and advance the Kingdom of Christ on earth together.

I hope that this century will be a golden age of Christian journey together.

About the Author

Peter Fields is proud to be an evangelical Protestant Christian. Fields grew up attending a strong evangelical Christian church and received a Christian school education. As he came to be involved in American social issues and political life, Fields came to develop a respect for the Roman Catholic Church and Catholic Christians and how they struggled to fight for Christian principles. He has decided to share his respect in print.